Teaching Play to Children with Autism

A Lucky Duck Book

Teaching Play to Children with Autism

A practical intervention using Identiplay

Nicky Phillips and Liz Beavan

Paul Chapman
Publishing

Paul Chapman Publishing
A SAGE Publications Company
1 Oliver's Yard
55 City Road
London EC1Y 1SP

SAGE Publications Inc.
2455 Teller Road
Thousand Oaks, California 91320

SAGE Publications India Pvt Ltd.
B 1/I 1 Mohan Cooperative Industrial Area
Mathura Road
New Delhi 110 044

SAGE Publications Asia-Pacific Pte Ltd
33 Pekin Street #02-01
Far East Square
Singapore 048763

Commissioning Editor: Barbara Maines

Editorial Team: Sarah Lynch, Mel Maines

Designer: Jess Wright

Illustrators: Phillipa Drakeford, Jess Wright

Library of Congress Control Number 2006937402

British Library Cataloguing in Publication data

A catalogue record for this book is available from the British Library

ISBN 978-1-4129-2894-6

Printed on paper from sustainable resources

Printed in Great Britain by The Cromwell Press Ltd, Trowbridge, Wiltshire

Contents

Acknowledgements

The authors would like to thank:

Jannik Beyer and Lone Gammeltoft for giving permission to develop their ideas.

Caroline Smith, Principal Educational Psychologist for Lincolnshire and the staff, pupils and parents of Riverside Community Special School.

Special thanks go to Jane Dabbs, Wendy Weaver, Margaret Gyngell, Kim Smith and Claire Gardiner.

Foreword

I have worked closely with the authors of this book over some years developing training events in the area of autism for parents and professionals. These events, open to all those living and working with children with autism, were inspirational. They were planned and delivered by parents, staff drawn from the school inspectorate service, teachers, classroom assistants, speech and language therapists and educational psychologists. The early training events drew on a range of commonly accepted interventions in autism including TEACCH, PECS and multi-element approaches to managing behaviours. Play was not included. Then one day there was a 'Eureka' moment when we sat and shared the obvious omission: 'Children are children; children with autism have the right to play too. Adults therefore will need to develop specific opportunities for children with autism.'

As a group we examined the literature, and as is still the case, the search revealed very little – less than ten books on developing play for children with autism.

The situation is a little better now. Evidence remains scarce on effective interventions. interventions which:

- enable children with autism to use toys in ways common to other children
- enable children with autism to hear and join in with play narratives
- enable children with autism to learn a play skill, generalise it and add to it creatively.

This book sets out one method of intervening in play. 'Identiplay' has a published, small evidence base regarding effective outcomes for children with autism. (Thomas and Smith, 2004).

In addition the authors make clear links between the skills necessary when children make a start on play and the skills developed by an Identiplay approach. It is so important that early approaches to play for children with autism rest on careful observation of the existing play skills of the child, the development of joint attention, the showing rather than telling of what play is, the use of simple story narratives and the use of visual structure. Identiplay focus on them all.

I am thrilled to see that professionals and parents are creatively developing specific interventions to enhance the play of children with autism. I am committed to developing the play of children with autism; put simply, it is what children do. I value this book which provides guidance of one way to start this journey.

For those who might read about Identiplay and question whether this particular method of 'teaching' play is too structured and whether it leads to the surface learning of meaningless routines, I must answer thus: Identiplay is a launch pad to some of the best work I have seen in the area of play for children with autism.

This book provides parents and professionals with the answer to a simple question, 'How might I make a start on play?' This book provides a practical starting place.

Dr Caroline Smith

Principal Educational Psychologist

Author of Writing and Developing Social Stories, Speechmark 2003

International trainer in the field of Language Impairment and Autism

What is in the pack and how to use it

There is a CD-ROM enclosed in this book. Some of the content of the book, shown on the page in black and white, is also available for printing out, sometimes in colour, for training or practitioner purposes. These resources include:

- play scripts
- video clips with text commentaries
- a PowerPoint file for training purposes.

The video and PowerPoint materials are suitable for projection onto a screen.

Section 1

Why Play?

Play

- *verb* 1. engage in games or other activities for enjoyment rather than for a serious or practical purpose
- *noun* 1. games and other activities engaged in for enjoyment.

Compact English Dictionary Online; Oxford University Press (2006)

The dictionary definition of play includes enjoyment as the key defining feature. It suggests that playing is about 'having a good time'.

Anyone who has spent time observing children in preschool and school settings, as well as at home, either as a professional or a parent, will have seen for themselves that play is an enjoyable activity. Smiles, laughter and shrieks of delight all feature in children's 'enjoyable' play.

Equally, those working or living with children will have heard youngsters' sadness explained by phrases such as, 'He won't play with me', 'She spoilt our game' or, 'I can't find anyone to play with.'

Enjoyment is clearly a key factor... but is there more to it? Is playing just about having fun? Research suggests that there is far more to play than that.

Early signs of play behaviour are evident in most children in the first months of life and follow a predictable developmental course. Babies engage in sensorimotor play, for example, banging or spinning objects and oral exploration from about three months of age. From 12 months, relational play is evident. This includes activities such as piling up toys or putting objects into things. Shortly after, at about 14 months, the first signs of pretend play develop in the form of functional play. This can be described as the appropriate use of an object or the conventional association of two or more objects, such as a spoon to feed a doll, or placing a teacup on a saucer. (Ungerer and Sigman, 1981) This stage is followed at 20 months by the beginnings of symbolic play, e.g. pretending that one object is something else.

While this pattern of development is evident in typically developing children, in children with autism these developmental stages of play are impaired and often absent.

Typically developing play has a number of distinct characteristics (Wolfberg, 1999):

- Firstly it is pleasurable, having a positive effect; children often smile and laugh when playing.
- Play requires active engagement. Children become absorbed in their play while they explore experiment and create. It is not an aimless activity.
- Play is voluntary and intrinsically motivated, as children freely choose the activity; motivation to play comes from within the child, with no external demands or rewards; it is self imposed, not imposed by others.
- Play involves attention to means over ends. In other words, there is a greater attention on the process of playing rather than what one 'gets out of it.' Any goals in play tend to be flexible, self directed and are changed frequently.
- Play is generally open ended.

- Play is flexible and changing. During play, children are free to do the unexpected; they can (and do) change the rules and experiment with new, untried behaviours and ideas. Play can change as children build on and alter their ideas.

- Finally, play tends to be nonliteral. In play, children treat objects, actions or events 'as if' they were something else; either using items as something completely different or playing at something real, e.g. 'play fighting.'

Play has been linked with advances in:

- cognitive

- social

- language

- emotional development.

(Rubin, Fein and Vandenberg, 1983). Wolfberg (1999) described the contribution that play makes to all these areas of a child's development.

Firstly, play is believed to contribute to and require a certain level of cognitive function. Children obtain knowledge of functional, spatial, causal and categorical relationships from early play activities as well as being introduced to thinking about meanings and limitations. In order to play, children, therefore, require a degree of flexibility and creativity in both their behaviour and their thinking. Both of these are also developed through play, leading to an increase and improvement in more original problem solving. Play also gives children an opportunity to experiment with new and unusual behaviour.

Play also develops social competence, through engaging in intimacy and affection, which often lead to the formation of friendships. Play requires negotiation and compromise and frequently requires the interpretation of subtle social cues. Play allows children to test out their ideas about possible relationships (Wolfberg, 1999).

Through play, children experiment with different forms of language and some of its rules. This experimentation leads to the development of new skills. The introduction of a narrative structure often begins during play and this later gives rise to a child's literary imagination. Playing encourages children to express themselves as individuals and helps them to interpret and make sense of the world (Wolfberg, 1999),

For most children, playing can also be a way of dealing with stress and upset in their lives and sometimes helps them to work through difficult times and experiences. It allows them to suspend reality and pretend to be someone or somewhere else.

Play in children with Autistic Spectrum Disorders

There is a general consensus that autism, or Autistic Spectrum Disorder, encompasses a set of three major diagnostic criteria which are closely connected to the main early observations of Leo Kanne and Hans Asperger, who first identified Autism and Asperger's syndrome respectively. These are delays in the areas of social relatedness, communication and behaviour and/or imagination. Traditionally these three main areas of delay are known as the 'triad of impairments'.

More recently it has been proposed that the 'triad' may be better described as developmental differences rather than impairment (Jordan et al, 2001). These are, after all, developmental areas not behaviours. Jordan suggested that the triad is social interaction, communication and flexibility in thinking and behaviour (not imagination); an essential desire to be in control. She proposed that children with autism do have some difficulties in creating something entirely from their imagination, but that that does not mean they cannot be exceptional artists in visual, musical or even the language arts. Cumine et al (2001) described the third impairment as 'social imagination and flexibility of thought.'

Children require a degree of flexibility and creativity in both their behaviour and their thinking in order to engage in play (Wolfberg, 1999). As deficits in this area of development are clearly evident in autism, this may offer an explanation as to why children with autism rarely engage in play.

Wolfberg (1999) describes the way in which children with autism tend to engage in more repetitive play, for example, manipulating objects, carrying out routines, lining objects up and following obsessive interests, with an emphasis on sensory stimulation. This behaviour is closely linked with the third part of the triad, namely impairment in 'imagination.' She argues that without specific teaching children with autism are unlikely to engage in functionally appropriate play.

In free play, children with autism also typically avoid or resist social interactions, tending towards watching others, playing alone or alongside their peers. They rarely initiate play themselves. (Wing and Attwood, 1987).

People play an important role in introducing children to the proper use of things, through joint attention and imitation. Williams (1998) argues that because children with autism tend not to include others in their use of objects, or use them to guide their own actions, they miss out on lots of information about how to use things in an appropriate way.

Similar arguments suggest that problems in using other people as a source of guidance for how to use objects may also account for reduced variety; without guidance from other people, children are left with their own, more limited ideas of interesting actions.

Children with autism do not join in with others in the typical shared pretend play situations but may show an ability to 'imagine' within their own narrow play routines. It is with sharing in the imagination of others and creating joint play scenarios that they have most difficulty, resulting in further difficulties in generalising learning to new situations, problem-solving and broadening interests outside the ones that dominate their thinking and behaviour.

Differences in the play of children with Autistic Spectrum Disorders and typically developing youngsters can affect the child's behaviour. As described previously, the benefits of play, which may be missed if a child with an autistic spectrum disorder is unable to independently engage in typical play behaviour, result in enhanced cognitive, social and emotional skills. Impairments or delays in these key areas are likely to result in challenging behaviour as the child attempts to communicate and get their needs met (Thornton & Cox, 2005).

Thornton and Cox (2005) ran individual play sessions with youngsters with Autistic Spectrum Disorders specifically to address challenging behaviour. They incorporated techniques which included rapport and relationships, imitation, gaining attention, turn-taking, enjoyment and structure. Their research found that such play interventions did impact on the children's behaviour, with a reduction in challenging behaviour following the structured play intervention.

In their work, Sherratt and Peter (2002) found that play activities tend to generate an emotional response, and will therefore target the part of brain that seems to be under functioning, according to some theories, in children with autism.

They maintain that play can be made to be memorable because it is fun, exciting, pleasurable and intriguing; sometimes even annoying and frustrating. They promote play-based approaches because they are live, energising and beneficial and hence tend to reinforce a sense of self. They create natural opportunities for children to access shared meaning within an experience. For these reasons, Sherratt and Peter (2002) suggest that play approaches and experiences are extremely important for children with Autistic Spectrum Disorders. They argue that simultaneously activating the areas of the brain associated with emotions and generative thought and explicitly teaching children with autism to play will lead to success. Sherratt and Peter (2002) call it the 'learning how to do it while doing it' approach. They say:

> In a rapidly changing, fast moving and culturally diverse world, if children with Autistic Spectrum Disorders are to be able to cope with and embrace the unexpected and unforeseen, and to have dealings with a diversity of people, then their capacity for creative, flexible, imaginative thinking needs to be developed. (p10)

The implications from the research are that children with autism require direct teaching of object function and toy use in structured situations. (Sherratt and Peter, 2002; Wolfberg, 1999)

What is Identiplay and where has it come from?

Research suggests that autistic children can learn 'play acts' if prompted. (Sherratt & Peter, 2002; Wolfberg, 1999; Libby et al, 1997) However, researchers have had to explore whether children are developing 'learned' behaviours or demonstrating genuine, spontaneous play behaviours.

Some of the studies do report generalisation to new settings, i.e. children using the new play skills in other situations, but one of the main issues is whether the play that is seen is an exact replication of the taught play, carried out with similar objects. Therefore, in some cases it is not clear whether the pretend play demonstrated after training relates to original ideas generated by the child (Neaum and Tallack, 1997). It appears possible to produce a string of play that looks imaginative and original, but may be a learned routine.

Sherratt and Peter (2002) explored this idea and suggested that initially the child may purely replicate the caregiver behaviour. However, they also report that this behaviour can develop into functional play by involving predictable play sequences and using explicit teaching. As the child's understanding develops, so the child may learn to engage in play with others and with more regard for the feelings and intentions of others. As a result, Sherratt and Peter (2002) identified key rules for teaching play sequences. These included:

- the use of simple narrative structure in any play sequence
- teachers leading the play.

They also argued that children should be assessed in free play prior to any intervention being put into place in order to establish a baseline and make realistic judgments about their abilities in play.

In their book, Autism and Play (2000), Beyer and Gammeltoft identify:

- shared focus
- imitation and mirroring
- parallel play
- play dialogue

as key elements when teaching play actions to children with autism. They recommended that during play sessions a 'stage' is set within a marked out place with recognisable toys that motivate. They also proposed that two sets of identical toys should be used so that the adult has the same as the child. This set up encourages all of the key elements listed above. Using parallel play, the adult mirrors the child at first, gradually introducing new ideas.

Sheratt (1999) emphasises the importance of a narrative structure. He suggests that it gives a reason, a framework and an end to the play act. The use of simple language, communicating affective as well as semantic meaning, is important. He also states that fun and excitement are crucial; that the adult has to play and enjoy it.

Setting up Tabletop Identiplay

Combining the key elements of these studies has led to the development of Identiplay, which can be described as consisting of:

- a table divided in two (using coloured sticky tape, if required) offering clearly separated areas for each set of toys
- two chairs set out face to face on either side of the table
- a pack containing two identical sets of toys (initially two or three toys of interest to the child which can be linked in a story form)
- a typed script detailing both the layout of the toys on the table, and what the adult will say and do with the toys.

It is vital that the child's free play is observed and her current skill level is noted before beginning to use Identiplay. This is in order to ensure that the toys chosen are appropriate to her play level. For example, a child who currently engages in sensory play, mouthing, pushing and pulling toys is not ready to be introduced to a doll with all her accessories. A more appropriate starting point might be a small car to push, or a piece of plasticine to roll out.

Once appropriate toys have been selected, the process begins with the adult setting out the two sets of toys on the table top, one set in each of the two areas of the table. The adult models the simple playscript, watching and waiting for the child's engagement. With some kits which are unfamiliar to the child, it may be helpful to give her a few minutes to explore the toys first.

In those situations in which the child does not engage, the adult may choose to put the toys away, saying, 'Play finished,' and repeat the process the next day, or it may be appropriate to prompt the child's involvement. This will depend on the individual child and how long she has been working with the adult already.

Initially the purpose of Identiplay is to increase the repertoire of toys with which the child will play. As the child becomes more familiar with the toys and creates her own play sequence, the adult joins the child's play, imitating her actions and sounds. It may be possible for the adult to sensitively add to the child's play, but he may need to revert back to mirroring or repeating the play sequence when additions are not welcomed by the child.

Before you start:

- Check the child's current play skills.
- Choose appropriate toys for her level.
- Make sure there is play script to accompany the toys.
- Set up the table and chairs.
- Let the child explore the toys if this is felt to be necessary.

Remember!

Identiplay can be used with youngsters of all ages as the toys and scripts are selected according to the child's level of play skills at that time. The authors have successfully used Identiplay with preschool children through to Key Stage 3 youngsters.

Why use Identiplay?

Identiplay facilitates many of the key elements found to be difficult for young children with Autistic Spectrum Disorder, i.e.

- shared focus
- imitation
- parallel play
- play dialogue
- narrative structure
- flexibility.

A recent small scale study (Thomas and Smith, 2004) looked at the effectiveness of Identiplay in helping children with autism develop play skills. The study involved preschool children and looked at three main questions.

Does Identiplay increase specific play behaviours?

Following daily use of Identiplay in a two week period, the data showed that the children:

- spent more time playing more appropriately with the tabletop toys
- learnt and used all or some of the taught Identiplay sequences.

Are these play behaviours then evident across different play contexts?

Analysis of video taken before and after the intervention identified that, after using Identiplay daily for a two week period:

- All of the children played more, and more purposefully, with the tabletop toys in free play sessions. For one child this reflected a shift from playing appropriately with a toy for 10% of the time to 100%.
- Similarly each child included, in some way, part of the taught play sequence. Two of the three used the taught sequence creatively, reproducing it in free play sessions and adding their own additional ideas to it.

Do the improved play behaviours lead to an increase in social interaction?

The post intervention evidence showed:

- an increase in the time spent by participant children playing alongside other children in parallel play and/or playing with other children
- microanalysis highlighted increased social interaction showed by frequency of eye contact and increase in verbal communication.

Some similar studies involving play interventions have found that post test behaviours were exact replicas of the training that each child had received (e.g. Libby et al, 1997). It can be speculated that the process of tabletop Identiplay, with its balance between skill teaching and mirroring, provides a sufficiently structured learning experience to not only start the play off, but also give the children enough confidence to do something new too.

Making your Identiplay kits – 12 Top Tips

1. Budget for the toys and allocate plenty of time to make them. Parent workshops can be a really useful way of getting parents together and getting work done.

2. The toys can be 'nearly identical', e.g. a yellow bowl and an orange bowl will be fine.

3. Choose durable toys and things that are easy for children to use (don't add to their frustration by using fiddly toys they can't manage).

4. £1 shops and supermarkets are a great source of Identiplay toys – you don't have to spend loads of money!

5. Gather toys from a range of places: cheap shops, supermarkets, car boot sales, give-aways, fast food outlets, free gifts and catalogues.

6. Some parts of the kits can be hand made, for example, a paper pond or cardboard tube tree.

7. Bag up the kits in 'zippy wallets' to keep the toys and scripts together.

8. Put different scripts onto different cards within each kit to make it easier for adults to follow.

9. Keep records – have a signing out system and if possible someone who coordinates this. This will help to keep track of the kits if lots of people are using them.

10. Always have some kits available, so that all children can access them and use them in their free play.

11. Try to introduce the kits in a distraction free environment.

12. Learn by your mistakes! Don't worry if things go wrong – just try again!

Section 2

Case Studies

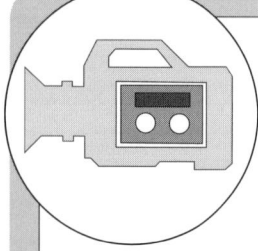

Who has used Identiplay?

Amy – a three old girl attending an inclusive mainstream preschool.

John – a boy aged nearly four who does not play.

Ben (video clip one) – a four year old boy with difficulty in social interaction.

Jack (video clip two) – a six year old boy with some difficult behaviours.

Luke (video clip three) – a boy with high anxiety levels.

Note: All the case studies are included on the CD-ROM as a printable resource.

Amy

Amy is a three old, attending an inclusive mainstream preschool. She has a diagnosis of autism and was extremely isolated in the setting.

At preschool, Amy's preferred activity was to sit alone at one end of the room picking small plastic fruits from a box and sorting them by colour, discarding the red ones by flinging them across the room. She occasionally picked up familiar books from the preschool and flicked the pages without looking at the book.

Amy is non verbal; that is, she has no functional language, and rarely showed awareness of any other people other than her own parents and siblings. None of the other children approached her as they had quickly learned that she ignored them and did not join in their play. She could also get aggressive if they came too close.

Amy's play leader decided to use Identiplay to introduce Amy to some new toys and how to use them. She used a small toy man with a wheelbarrow and some tools, and during Amy's individual intervention time each morning she played out a little script with the tools going into the wheelbarrow ('in!') and the man moving forward ('Push, push, push!'). The script had a great deal of potential for extension, but given Amy's lack of play skills at the start, the key worker chose a simple sequence initially.

After about a week of sharing the Identiplay kit and script with Amy, the play leader noted that Amy started to copy the actions, not clearly but definitely touching and pushing the toy. The toys from the kit were put out at free play time for Amy to use if she chose; however initially she continued with her routine of sorting the red fruits from the others.

After two weeks of using Identiplay, Amy was observed in the preschool free play time picking up the toys from the kit and pushing the man and wheelbarrow, as in the script. She did this for a few seconds at a time at first before continuing with her sorting activity, however, after a few days, Amy was spending longer putting the tools in the wheelbarrow and pushing it. One day, just a few days after she started to do this, a couple of other girls came over to her and sat alongside, watching her play. As she pushed the toys, they too tried to join in, and leaning in towards her one of them tickled her. Amy laughed and looked at her. From this followed several minutes of social play between the girls, e.g. tickling, lap games, etc.

Amy continued to use Identiplay kits, adding more sequences as she learned and used new ones. She remains largely non verbal and still prefers her own activities much of the time. However, she does play with script toys in the setting and her peers join in with her play, and she tolerates and increasingly enjoys that.

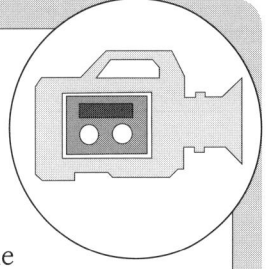

John

John was almost four. He went to preschool and had a diagnosis of classic autism. John had no functional language and did not play either at preschool or at home. John spent his time walking around, flapping his hands and humming. He did not like other people near him and his behaviour could be challenging. John showed very little awareness of others around him, and did not demonstrate shared attention at all.

Each day John spent some time with his key worker, working on tolerating others and sensory awareness. She used massage and sensory toys to try to engage him. John did enjoy some of the toys, like the bubbles, but mostly appeared to ignore what was happening around him.

The key worker decided to introduce some plasticine as a new sensory experience, and chose to follow the principles of Identiplay. She took two balls of plasticine and two rollers and each day rolled her plasticine, singing 'Roll, roll, roll' as she passed the roller over it several times. Each day John sat and looked around him as if nothing was happening, without looking, let alone touching any of the toys.

After a couple of weeks, with no change at all, the key worker had almost decided to give up with the Identiplay when a visitor called in to the play session to see how they were getting on. After seeing the Identiplay, and John seemingly not taking any notice at all, the visitor started discussing the intervention with the key worker. She stopped rolling and started talking to the visitor about Identiplay, John's programme and how she was probably going to give up using the plasticine.

As they talked they suddenly became aware of a small noise. Looking around they were amazed (and delighted!) to see John had picked up the roller and was rolling his plasticine, singing (in a very tiny voice!) 'Roll, roll, roll!'

I know this lovely story is true because I was the visitor! I think it is a great reminder to persevere for just a bit longer, even when the situation may be feeling hopeless.

Ben – video clip one

Ben is a four year old boy with a probable diagnosis of autism. (He received a diagnosis of classic autism a year later.) Ben, at the time of making the video, was on the Thomas Outreach Programme (TOP). TOP offers support to preschool children with significant social interaction and communication difficulties, both within the home and within the preschool setting.

Prior to receiving support Ben presented with challenging behaviour. Much of this was felt to be directly related to the fact that he had severely restricted functional communication and was unable to express his needs effectively. In addition to this, he was at his most relaxed when engrossed in one of his preferred activities – playing with his trains or using the computer. When involved in an activity of this kind he was particularly hard to reach and was likely to have a temper tantrum if interrupted.

Ben had been receiving support both within his home and at pre-school for several months prior to the videoing. He had been introduced to the Picture Exchange Communication System (PECS) which had given him a voice. He was using the TEACCH principle (Schopler) and had a visual timetable/schedule and independent work system. The schedule was enabling him to access more activities at both home and pre-school and had helped to reduce his temper tantrums. He had also been having Special Time (Cockerill).

The video clip shows Ben on the day he was introduced to Identiplay. He is in his home and is working with his TOP worker.

It is important to note that when children are introduced to the approach they may engage in it for a very short space of time – this is fine. It is possible to extend the time children will engage in the activity by building in a regular time to do it and developing the complexity of the script.

It is important to engage the child in play that is matched to their play level. If a child is still at a stage where their play involves much sensory exploration, they will not be ready for the play experience being introduced to Ben.

As the video is viewed it will be noticed that the play equipment that Ben is using is not very stable and falls apart. Ben is very tolerant and tries to put the equipment back together and he is then helped by his TOP worker. The importance of choosing suitable equipment cannot be over emphasised – Ben was very tolerant, other children may not be.

It may be possible to engage the child by choosing equipment that is known to be of high interest to him. However, there needs to be a word of caution – equipment of high interest may result in the child becoming extremely self-absorbed and this may make it difficult to move the play forward. The importance of observation as an assessment tool cannot be over-stated as this often will provide the information that is so essential to the planning of an effective teaching intervention.

Discussion: Ben's clip shows him doing Identiplay for the first time. Before beginning any intervention it is essential to assess the child's level in order to pitch the activities correctly. Discuss how you might have assessed Ben's play levels prior to beginning Identiplay. What would you do? What resources might you use?

Jack – video clip two

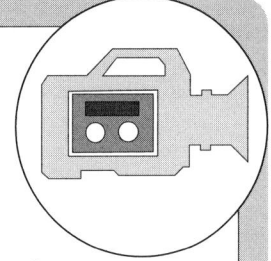

Jack attends a school for children with learning difficulties. He has a diagnosis of classic autism. In addition to this he has severe and complex learning needs. Jack has been in specialist provision since he was a pre-school child. He is now in year one and is six years old.

Jack has benefited from being in a school that provides him with good routines, a work environment that promotes visual clarity and a highly consistent approach to the management of his behaviour – Jack can be aggressive towards adults.

Although Jack has verbal language he uses PECS to enable him to extend his skills and knowledge. PECS has been particularly helpful when he is working in a small group in which he has to take turns and communicate with his peers. Jack also uses the TEACCH principle (Schopler) – he has a visual schedule and an independent work system.

Jack has been doing Identiplay for some time. Initially he did not respond to the wording on the script and it was necessary to add sound effects to cue and stimulate his responses.

It is interesting to note that during the session Jack makes several requests for the activity to be continued. He also looks towards the adult on several occasions to check that is he was doing was correct. This was most noticeable when he is finding a particular coloured door or key. What we know about Jack is that he can match colour but does not associate a colour with its name.

Discussion: Jack asks to continue the activity several times, which is great! Some children however may request something over and over again, and it's possible that it may then become difficult to stop or change the activity. Discuss how you might move on a child in this situation while still encouraging them to enjoy the activity.

Luke – video clip three

Luke has a diagnosis of classic autism and he suffers from high levels of anxiety. In school he often appears to be coping well, however quite often when he gets home the situations he has found difficult in school impact on the life of the family. Luke's anxiety can present itself as quite challenging behaviour in the home situation. This perhaps emphasises the need to work in close partnership with parents.

The video clip shows Luke making a glass of squash. As this was going to be a new experience for Luke it was decided to rehearse the script and play scenario prior to videoing with the hope that we would reduce any of his anxieties. As the video clip is played it becomes very apparent that this one rehearsal has been rapidly memorised and Luke is quick to prompt the teacher, reminding her that there is ice in the freezer.

When we had finished videoing, Luke completely re-enacted the phases the teacher went through to clear away the activity and set it up ready for videoing. Many children like Luke do show this unusual skill.

Discussion: How would you begin to move Luke on to generalising this life skill? Where and how would you try generalisation and what resources might be useful?

Section 3

Kits and Scripts

Layout of Kits

1. Cars
2. Animal Set
3. Click-clack Cars
4. Animal Train
5. Children's Playground
6. Farmyard
7. Garages
8. The Sea
9. Dolls
10. Dog with Pet Carrier
11. Building Blocks
12. Space Shuttle
13. Firemen.

Layout of Kits

Assemble each kit with two sets of toys, identical or very similar. 13 examples showing one detail of the toy kit are given in this section of the book and on the CD-ROM.

Ideally the two kits can then be set out opposite each other for face-to-face play.

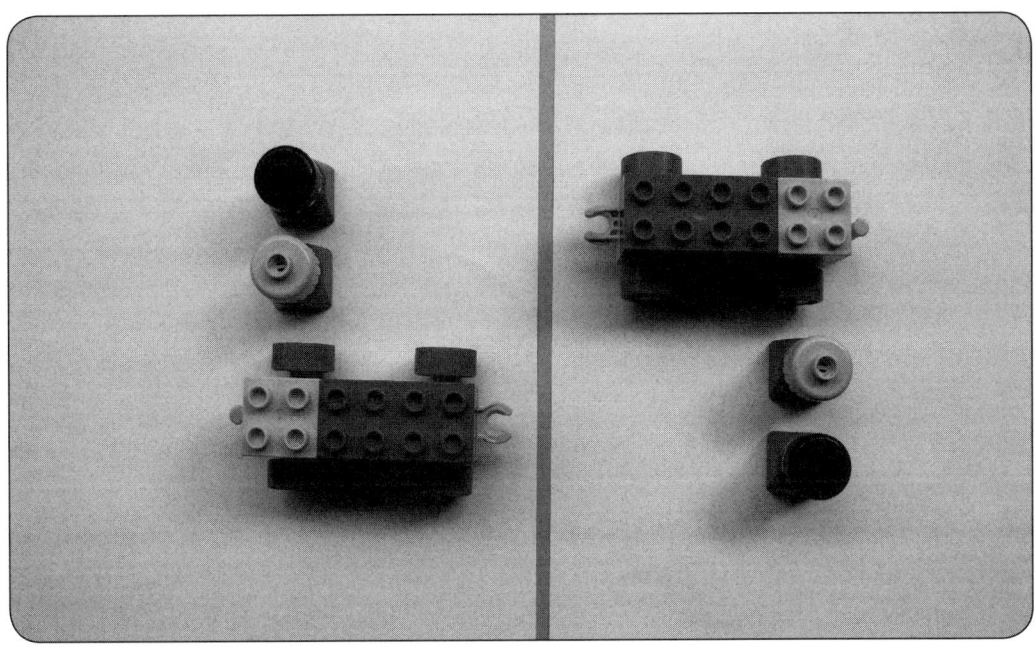

Sometimes side by side play is more comfortable for the young person

Cars

This kit contains:

- two toy cars

- four play people.

Script

Put one person on the car and say, 'Man on car'.

Push car along table and say, 'Push car, brrm, brrm.'

Say, 'Finished.'

Extension

Introduce the other person.

Carry out the previous script.

Drive the car to the other person and stop beside them. Say, 'Stop the car'.

Make the first person get off the car and say, 'Man off car'.

Say, 'Hello friend! Come with me.'

Put people back on car and say, 'Two men in car'.

Push car and say, 'Push car; brrm, brrm'.

'Finished.'

Animal Set

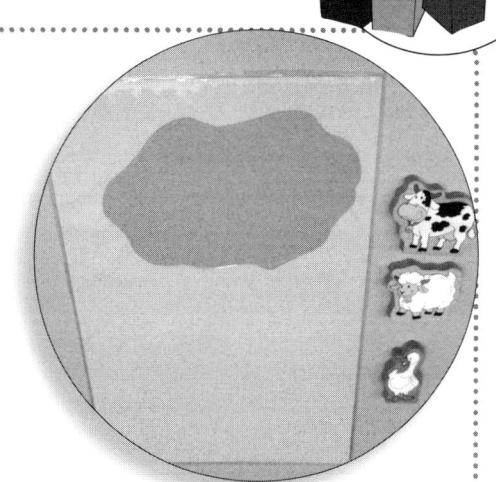

This kit contains:

- two cows
- two sheep
- two ducks
- two pieces of green card with a blue paper pond.

Script

Move the cow onto the field (green card) and say, 'Cow – walk walk walk'.

Move sheep onto field and say, 'Sheep – walk, walk, walk'.

Move duck across field and into pond and say, 'Duck – walk, walk, splash'.

Say, 'Finished.'

Click-clack Cars

This kit contains:

- two click clack runs

- two sets of cars

  (green, red, blue, yellow).

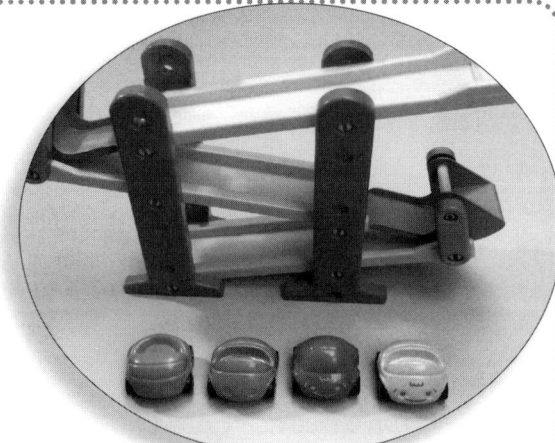

Script

Begin by using one car only. Put car at top and push it down and say, 'Car down – click clack, click clack.'

Say, 'Finished.'

Extension

Introduce the other cars and put them down the run one after another.

You may want to introduce colours and numbers as part of this script depending on the age and ability of the child, for example, 'Red car down', or 'Find the (red) car', or 'One car down, two cars down,' etc.

Animal Train

This kit contains:

- two trains with carriages

- two zebras

- two lions

- two elephants.

Script

Introduce the train and say, 'Push train – choo, choo choo.'

Say, 'Finished'.

Extension

Introduce other pieces of equipment one at a time as the child becomes confident with the previous one.

When introducing carriages say, 'Clickety clack, clickety clack.'

Introduce the animals and say, 'Put (elephant) into carriage.'

Further extension

Combine the scripts, for example, 'Put (elephant) into carriage – clickety clack, clickety clack,'or 'Push elephant in train – choo, choo, choo.'

Children's Playground

This kit contains:

- two slides

- two see saws

- two swings

- two families of mum, dad, boy and girl.

Script

Begin with one of the people and the slide.

Make the person go up the slide and say, 'Up, up, up.'

Move the person down the slide and say, 'Down, wheee.'

Say, 'Finished.'

Extension

Introduce another person and the see saw.

Put the people on the see saw and say, 'On the see saw.'

Move them up and down and say, 'Up and down, up and down.'

Include the initial script with the slide.

Further extension

Use the previously introduced equipment and scripts and introduce the final two people and the swings.

Put a person on the swing and make one of the people push them, saying, 'Push, push, swing.'

The play equipment on the swing can also be introduced with commentary such as, 'Up, up, up' for the ladder and, 'Swing, swing,' for the hoops.

Farmyard

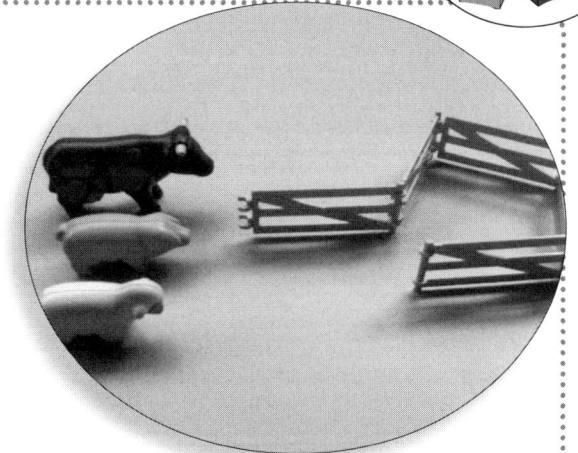

This kit contains:

- two cows
- two sheep
- two pigs
- two fences.

Script

Make the fence into an enclosed pen with a small gap to enter by.

Move cow into the pen and say, 'Cow – walk in – moo.'

Move sheep into pen and say, 'Sheep – walk in – baa.'

Move pig into pen and say, 'Pig – walk in – oink.'

Say, 'Finished.'

Extension

Once familiar with this script, you may want to try saying, 'Find the (cow)', before the child carries out that part of the play sequence.

Garages

This kit contains:

- two garages
- two cars
- two sets of keys.

Script

With this kit, if the child has difficulty with using the keys, leave doors unlocked to begin with.

If using the keys, unlock the doors and say, 'Unlock first door.'

Say, 'Car out,' and move the car out of the garage.

Drive the car around the garage and say, 'Round you go, brrm, brrm.'

Stop car at door; say, 'Stop car, in you go.'

Drive the car into the garage and lock the door; say, 'Shut door; bye bye car.'

Say, 'Finished.'

Extension

Introduce the colours and include in script; e.g. 'Red car out', 'Bye bye blue car', etc.

Further extension

Take the cars out and park in a line. Ask the child to find the (red) car.

The Sea

This kit contains:

- two beach/sea picture mats
- two figures
- two crabs
- two fish.

Script

Each of these steps can be carried out individually or put together as a whole script, depending on the age and ability of the child.

Move a figure from beach to water's edge; say, 'Walk, walk, walk.'

Put a figure in the water and make them move their leg; say, 'Splash, splash, splash.'

Move the fish along the mat; say, 'Swim, swim, swim.'

Make the figure point to the fish; say, 'Look! Fish!'

Move a crab to a figure; say, 'Pinch, pinch, pinch.'

Make the figure jump up and down; say, 'Ouch, ouch, ouch!'

Say, 'Finished.'

Dolls

This kit contains:

- two dolls
- two bottles
- two dummies
- two bowls with spoons.

Script

Begin with only the doll. Hold the doll in your arms and rock it. Say, 'Rock baby to sleep.' You can introduce actions such as kissing the baby, hugging the baby, etc. Name the actions as they are done, e.g. 'Aaahh, hug the baby.'

Extension

Introduce the other equipment gradually, as the child becomes confident with the previous things.

Give the bottle to the doll; say, 'Give baby a drink, mmm.'

Spoon food from the bowl into the doll's mouth; say, 'Mmm, baby's hungry,' or, 'Give baby food.'

Put the dummy in the doll's mouth; say, 'Night night, baby.'
Rock the doll as before.

Dog with Pet Carrier

This kit contains:

- two toy dogs
- two pet carriers.

Script

Start with the dog out of the pet carrier. Say, 'Dog is ill. Poor dog.'

Stroke the dog.

Put dog in the carrier. Say, 'Dog in carrier. Let's go to the vet.'

Carry the dog in the carrier and pretend to go to the vet.

Extension

Continue this into a role play of being at the vet, e.g. get dog out of carrier. Say, 'Hello vet, my dog is ill. Poor dog.'

Stroke the dog. Say, 'Can I have some medicine for my dog?'

Put the dog back in the carrier. Say, 'Thank you vet. Good bye.'

Building Blocks

This kit contains:

- two green blocks

- two red blocks

- two blue blocks

- two yellow blocks with eyes

- two small yellow blocks.

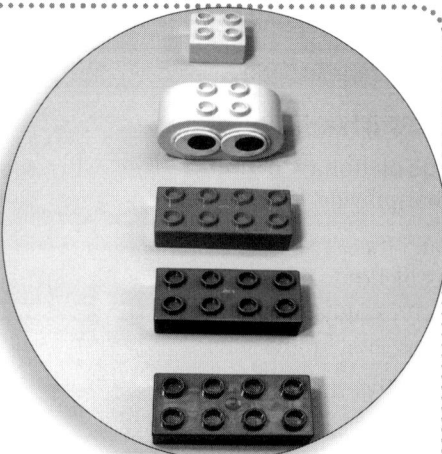

Script

Build with the blocks putting one on top of the other. Say, 'Green brick on', 'Red brick on', 'Face on' etc.

Say, 'Finished.'

Extension

Once familiar with this activity, it can be given as an independent task, using a picture cue, as below, to prompt.

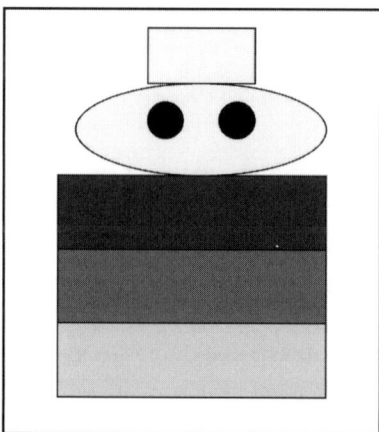

Space Shuttle

This kit contains:

- two space shuttles

- two spacemen

- two space buggies.

Script

Begin with man and buggy in space shuttle. Make space shuttle take off and fly; say, 'Take off, brrrm, brrrm; fly to space.'

Depending on the child's age and ability you may like to introduce the countdown, ie., '5,4,3,2,1, take off.'

Extension

Fly the space shuttle and land it on the table; say, 'Land on the moon.'

Open the doors, saying, 'Open doors.'

Take the man out and say, 'Man out.'

Move the man around the space shuttle; say, 'Walk on the moon.'

Return the man into the shuttle and say, 'Man in.'

Fly the shuttle again as before.

Further extension

Use the previous scripts and introduce the buggy. Put the man in the buggy and drive him around as part of the script. Say, 'Man in buggy, drive on the moon.'

Firemen

This kit contains:

- two sets of:

- a fire engine
- four firemen
- fire extinguisher
- oxygen cylinder
- axe

- a walkie talkie
- a megaphone
- card door
- card fire
- card dog.

Script

Put two firemen in driving seats and two on the back of the engine. Say, 'Let's go!'

Drive engine along table; say, 'Nee naw, nee naw.'

Take the firemen off the back, fix the hose and the ladder.

Firemen climb the ladder; say, 'Up, up, up.'

Firemen aim hose; say, 'Squirt, squirt, squirt; fire's out.'

Firemen down ladder; say, 'Down, down, down.'

Put the ladder and hose away and drive the engine back across table. Say, 'Finished.'

Extension

Introduce the rest of the equipment and the card fire, door and dog. Give the axe to one fireman, the fire extinguisher to another and the oxygen and walkie talkie to the third. The remaining fireman is the chief.

Make the chief fireman say, 'Break down the door.'

Make first fireman hit the door with the axe; say, 'Go in.' Turn door over.

Second fireman used the fire extinguisher on the fire; say, 'Squirt, it's out.' Turn the fire over.

Third fireman says, 'Let's go dog!' Make the fireman take the dog and say, 'Mission accomplished!' Say, 'Finished.'

Section 4

Identiplay Beyond the Tabletop

The potential of the approach would appear to be endless. In this chapter some of the activities that have been used to develop children's play skills in other commonly found play opportunities will be presented.

The ultimate goal of Identiplay is to enable children with ASDs to access play in the appropriate learning area of the setting. To this end it is important to remember that the equipment used during the teaching session should then be placed in the learning area. By doing this the child or children are provided with the opportunity to generalise the play skills that have been taught in the learning area.

Within the teaching session many of the children who have been given systematic or structured teaching using the approach have shown their ability to take the lead in the play. This is an activity which, initially, was very much teacher led being taken forward by the child herself.

Within the chapter there will be presented some examples of play scripts used with some young children with complex learning needs. Following this there are some examples of play scenarios that have been developed for use in other play areas, for example, the sand tray.

Both sand and water play are popular activities with typically developing children and those with ASDs alike. However, observations made over time have led to the conclusion that many of the children with ASDs become involved in a range of stereotypical play – flicking, patting or watching the water or sand trickle from containers. This pattern of behaviour being repeated many times over often has the potential to isolate the child as she becomes absorbed in the activity. It cannot be denied that for many children this type of activity does fulfil a purpose, for example, it may serve to calm a child who has become agitated. At other times, this highly repetitive type of activity may serve to self-stimulate some children making it more difficult for them to move onto the next activity or reduce the potential to access learning when they have been successfully transitioned to the next activity. It may be that for some children, their more limited use of imagination restricts their ability to explore these learning opportunities comprehensively.

Ducks and Water

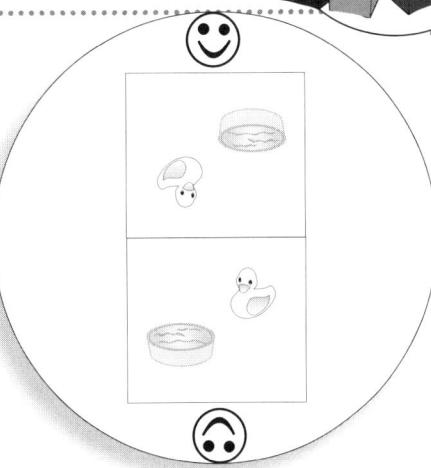

Equipment

- two plastic ducks
- two bowls or baths containing a small amount of water.

Script

'Duck in bath.'

'Splash, splash, splash.'

'Duck out of bath.'

'Finished.'

Top Tips

To enable some young children to access this type of activity and build their tolerance to it, as well as increasing their ability to persist at an activity for a longer period of time, it may be helpful to use a sand-timer to timeframe the activity.

Many young with children with an ASD do not have a concept of 'finished', it is, therefore, important to teach this concept.

In some instances and in the early stages of development, some young children may require physical prompting to access this type of activity. It is important to explain this to parents or carers before this is done.

Puppet Play

Equipment

- two puppets.

Script

(Place puppet on hand, raise hand and start to look at the puppet.)

'Hello, I'm .... What's your name?'

(Move the puppet to your ear as if listening to its response.)

'How old are you?'

(Repeat the action as if listening to the puppet – continue having a conversation with the puppet.)

Puppets can be used to have any number of conversations, but it is also useful to add a range of props and work with the puppet to 'play out' play scenarios, for example, writing a note, drinking a cup of tea or washing a dolly.

Top Tips

Some children may find talking to adults or children in direct conversation extremely difficult. Using a puppet to have a conversation not only models the process of having a conversation but also provides opportunities to begin to make conversations with the child.

Many speech and language programmes involve teaching the child a range of verbs, prepositions etc. Puppet play provides an ideal opportunity to undertake this work.

Working with Play Dough

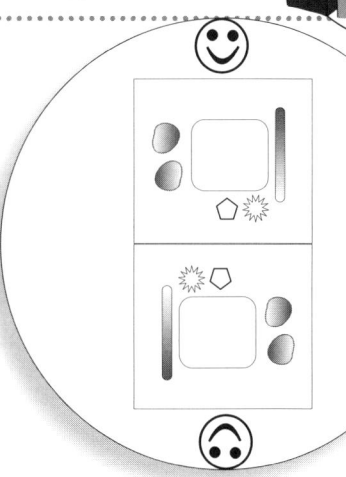

Equipment

- two play mats
- two rollers
- two matching balls of play dough
- two cutters.

Script

(Place the play dough in the centre of the play mat and pick up the roller.) 'Roll, roll, roll.'

(Use the roller to flatten the ball of play dough.) Repeat the phrase, 'Roll, roll, roll,' until the play dough is flattened and approximately 1cm in thickness.

'Roller down.' (Put the roller down.)

'Shape.' (Pick up the shape and place it in the centre of the play dough.)

'Press, press.' (Using your hand to press the shape into the play dough.)

'Shape out.' (Lift the shape carefully from the play dough and put it to the side of the play mat.)

'Pick up the shape.' (Carefully remove the play dough from around the edge of the shape and lift the shape up.)

'Look, it's a ....' (Look at the shape and smile.)

Working at the Sand Tray

In the early stages of play with sand it is likely that a young child will be encouraged to fill buckets and make sandcastles. This activity, readily, lends itself to an Identiplay type of activity.

Making Sandcastles

Equipment

- two buckets
- two spades
- sand tray containing 'wet' sand
- tape or cane to divide the tray into two play areas
- two sets of play moulds.

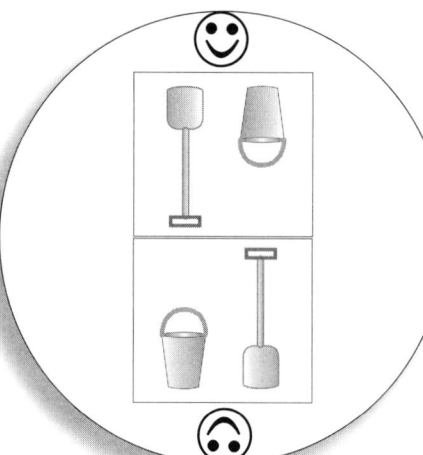

Script

'Sand in bucket.'

'Pat, pat, pat.'

'Pick it up.'

'Over it goes.'

'Pat, pat, pat.'

'Lift it up.'

'Hurray – a castle.'

Top Tips

Some children with ASDs may find playing in or with sand difficult as they find the 'feel' of the sand unpleasant. To enable them to overcome this difficulty it may be possible to provide them with rubber gloves to wear during the activity.

Some children may be very reluctant to play with sand at all. However, if a child has a particular interest in, for example, stars, as was the case with one of the children in the setting, making stars in the sand tray using a mould may enable him to access this resource.

Working at the Sand Tray (cont.)

Generally one would stand opposite the child, either at opposite ends or sides of the sand tray. Some children with ASDs may find this difficult – in such instances standing side by side with the child may prove to be successful.

Some children with ASDs find working in the close proximity of others difficult, a situation that could easily occur when young children choose to play at or in the sand tray. Usually pre-school practitioners or teachers restrict the number of children accessing this learning opportunity at any one time. In addition, it may be helpful, in the initial stages of more generalised learning, to mark the space each child has to stand in and create play zones within the tray itself. As the child with an ASD becomes more able to manage the proximity of others then these 'restrictions' can be systematically reduced until they are all removed.

More advanced sand play

In much the same way that miniature world characters or equipment is used to extend the child's imaginative play through the tabletop activities previously outlined, then so it is possible to create similar play scenarios within the sand tray or builders' tray.

Moving Sand, Rocks or Tree Trunks

Equipment

- two diggers

- two lorries

- two sets of small rocks

- two sets of miniature logs or tree trunks.

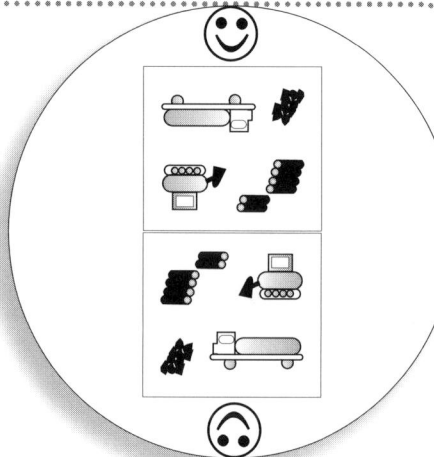

Script

'Sand, rocks or tree trunks in digger.' (Lower bucket of digger, load with one of the materials.)

'Up, up.' (Raise the bucket.)

'Digger to lorry.' (Drive the digger to the lorry.)

'Stop.'

'Sand, rocks or tree trunks in the lorry.' (Lower the bucket and empty the sand, rocks or tree trunks into the lorry.)

'Off we go.' (Drive the lorry around the sand or builders' tray.)

'Stop.'

'Sand out.' (Empty the load from the lorry.)

It may be possible to repeat the activity using the other materials. However, this is very much dependent upon the attention span of the child.

As with all Identiplay activities, the sand tray or builders' tray should be divided into two equal sections. The equipment is then laid out in an identical manner in each of the sections.

Top Tips

Many children with ASDs have high levels of interest in some pieces of equipment, for example, characters from popular children's books or cartoon characters. These interests may be successfully used to engage the child in play and, therefore, move the play forward. However, this high level of interest may mean that the child becomes very absorbed in their own activity making it difficult to engage her in any other activity. The key to success is 'knowing' and understanding the needs of the child. An informal assessment, using short periods of observation, will serve to identify resources that will readily engage the child and those that result in high levels of self-absorption which make it hard to teach her.

More Identiplay Activities for the Sand Tray

- Buried treasure.
- Making tunnels.
- Making tracks or trails using vehicles, animal footprints.
- Creating patterns or letter shapes with lollipop sticks.
- Drawing simple pictures in wet sand, for example, a face.

Children, as is known, are at very different stages in their development. It is therefore important to prepare play scripts related to play scenarios at varying levels. Presented below is one of the very earliest scripts used.

Top Tips

To enable some young children to access this type of activity and build their tolerance to it, as well as increasing their ability to persist at an activity for a longer period of time, it may be helpful to use a sand timer to timeframe the activity.

Many young with children with an ASD do not have a concept of 'finished'; it is, therefore, important to teach this concept.

In some instances and in the early stages of development, some young children may require physical prompting to access this type of activity. It is important to explain this to parents or carers before this is done.

Working in the Water Tray

Observation of many children with ASDs at play in the water tray has shown that this popular activity often gives rise to stereotypical play. Splashing created by the flapping of the hands in the water is very common. However, when presented with a range of small boats, several of the children appeared to lack the imagination to use these toys in ways that typically developing children usually do.

Playing with Boats

Equipment

- two small boats

- two miniature figures

- one water tray, preferably with a small ledge.

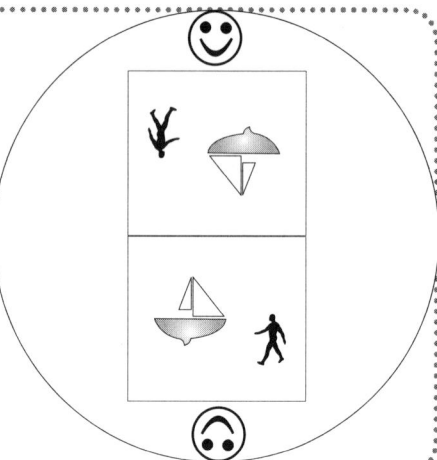

Script

'Man in boat.'

'Off we go.'

(Steer the boat back to the starting point.)

'Man out of boat.'

Helicopter Rescue

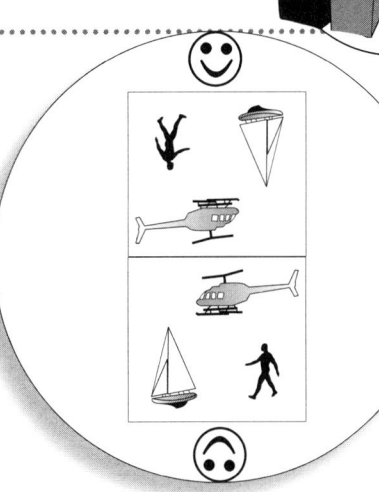

Equipment

- two helicopters, simple ladders, miniature figures

- two boats with miniature figures on board.

Script

'The man is sailing in his boat.' (Gently push the boat through the water.)

'The wind is starting to blow and the water is getting rough.' (Bob the boat up and down in the water.)

'The boat is tipped over.' (Tip the man out of the boat into the water.)

'The man shouts for help – Help! Help! Help!'

'The helicopter flies to the man.' (Put the pilot in the helicopter and fly it to the man in the water.)

'The helicopter gets to the man, the pilot lowers the ladder and climbs down to rescue the man in the water.' (Lower the ladder, 'climb' the pilot down the ladder, pick up the man from the water and climb up the ladder into the helicopter.)

'The helicopter flies back to where it started.'

'The man is rescued.' (Get the man out of the helicopter.)

Diving for Treasure

Equipment

- two figures dressed for swimming

- two treasure chests or boxes that can be submerged in the water tray

- two selections of small items – coins, jewellery, etc.

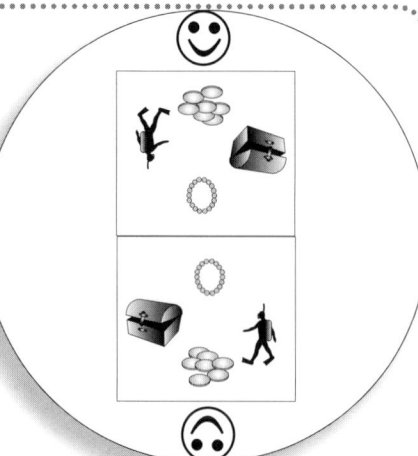

Script

'The man dives into the water.' (Have the man standing on the side of the water tray and 'dive' him into the water.)

'He swims to the sunken treasure.' ('Swim' the man through the water until he is above the treasure.)

'He dives under the water and collects the treasure.' ('Dive' the man under the water and collect the treasure.)

'The man swims back to the shore and puts his treasure down.'

Top Tips

Many children with ASDs find creative or imaginative writing difficult. Identiplay can be used as the stimulus for this type of work. Preparing a vocabulary list or word grid using a computer program prior to the task has also been shown to remove some of the barriers associated with writing and so has made the writing experience much more productive.

Section 5

Using Identiplay With Other Resources

Using Identiplay with Other Resources

It has often been reported that children with ASDs play with popular play resources in unusual ways. For example, it would not be unusual to see a child placing all the toy cars in a line, or lying on the floor watching the wheels rotate or merely spinning the wheels of a car. The typically developing child is likely to create his own play scenario when using this type of play equipment. It may be that they are re-enacting the journey to school in the morning or it may be that they are creating an elaborate play scenario involving emergency vehicles. As the play evolves other children may become involved in the scenario.

Play is very much a social process and has the potential to support the development of the essential social communication skills used in most group learning situations, for example, sharing, turn-taking, negotiating and making compromises. For many children with ASDs these skills have to be taught and then generalised. Identiplay, while not providing all of the answers, does begin to equip the child with a play scenario that will enable him to begin to 'get in on the act'.

The Car Mat

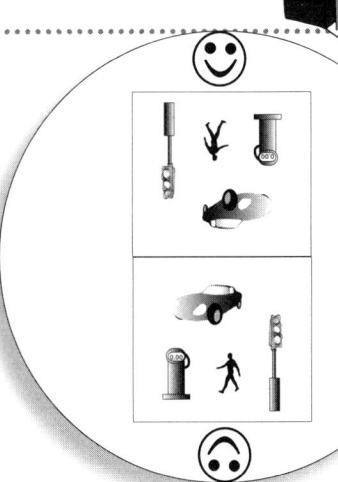

Equipment

- two small car mats
- two small cars
- two miniature figures
- two miniature petrol pumps or traffic lights.

Script

'The man is driving his car along the road, he is going to the garage to get some petrol.' (Push the car along the road.)

'The car turns to the right.'

'The man sees the traffic lights the lights are red. He has to stop the car.' (Continue to push the car and make it turn to the right, push it up to the traffic lights, bring it to a stop.)

'The man drives on, he turns to the left and drives on to the garage.'

'He fills the car with petrol.' (Use the miniature figure to pretend to put petrol in the car.)

'The man pays for the petrol.'

'He drives his car to the shops and parks his car before he goes shopping.'

The Car Mat (cont.)

The car mat can be used for a vast number of play scenarios. However, it is important to:

- create scripts for each scenario

- ensure that the language used in the script matches the language level of the child with whom it is being used

- staff being asked to work with the child are conversant with the appropriate script.

Top Tips

Quite often children with ASDs have programmes from a speech and language therapist. They may also have programmes from an occupational therapist and, possibly, a physiotherapist too. One of the most frequently asked questions is, 'How do I fit it all in?' There is no easy answer to this question. However, play often provides the parent or practitioner with the opportunity to practise the exercises from the child's programmes in a meaningful and fun way. Without a doubt, play provides opportunities to extend the child's vocabulary and knowledge of a vast array of key concepts.

More Identiplay activities using play mats

Similar play scenarios and scripts can be written involving a variety of play mats:

- flights from the airport

- dinosaur adventures

- a trip to the zoo

- at the farm

- creating a town or village

- a simple train set can be used in much the same way as the play mats.

Planting a Seed

Equipment

- two watering cans
- two pairs of gloves
- two pebbles
- two plant pots
- two plant pot saucers
- two pieces A4 card

- two trowels
- two seed packets
- two tubs of compost
- two plant labels
- two pens
- two cloths

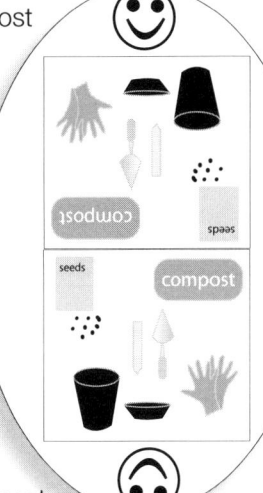

Script

Fill the watering can with cold water.

Put on the gloves.

Put the pebble in the bottom of the plant pot.

Pick up the trowel use it to half fill the plant pot with compost.

Open the packet of seeds and count out three seeds.

Put the seeds on the compost in the plant pot.

Sprinkle the seeds with water.

Use the trowel to cover the seeds with compost.

Sprinkle the compost in the plant pot with water.

Take off the gloves.

Pick up the plant label and pen.

Read the name of the seeds written on the packet of seeds.

Place the label on the table and copy the names of the seeds onto the label with the pen.

Push the label into one side of the plant pot so that the name of the seeds can be read.

Carry the plant pot and the plant pot saucer to the window sill.

Place the saucer on the window sill then stand the plant pot on the saucer.

Return to your work area, take the piece of card and fold it in half. Use the pen to write a notice that says: 'Remember to water the seeds'.

Take the notice to the windowsill and stand it close by the plant pots.

Return to your work area, tidy up your equipment.

Use the wet cloth to wipe the work surface.

Laying the Table

Equipment

- two place mats

- two forks

- two knives

- two spoons

- two napkins.

Script

Take the place mat and put it on the table, in front of the chair and close to the edge of the table.

Pick up the knife and put it on the place mat close to the right hand side of the place mat.

Pick up the fork and put it on the place mat close to the left hand side of the place mat.

Pick up the spoon and put it on the place mat between the knife and fork.

Making a Glass of Squash

Equipment

- two jugs
- two glasses
- two bottles of the child's preferred fruit squash
- access to a tap to get water
- access to a freezer in which ice-cubes can be stored.

Script

Go to the tap and fill the jug with cold water then take the jug to the work area.

Take the glass and put it near the jug.

Take the bottle of fruit squash and unscrew the cap on the bottle.

Hold the glass steady and use the other hand to lift the bottle and pour a small quantity of the fruit squash into the glass.

Put the bottle down and screw the top back on then move it to the side.

Hold the glass steady, pick up the jug with the other hand, pour some water into the glass and keep pouring until the glass is nearly full.

Put the jug down and to the side.

Go to the freezer, open the door and take out the tray of ice-cubes then carry the tray of ice-cubes back to the work area.

Turn the ice-cube tray over and tap the bottom of the tray then add three of the ice cubes to the glass of fruit squash.

Drink the squash.

Clear away the equipment and wash up the glass.

Making a Sandwich

Equipment

- two chopping boards
- two knives
- four slices of bread
- two tubs of butter-like spread
- two pots of the child's favourite sandwich filling
- two teaspoons
- two plates
- two napkins.

Script

Place the chopping board on a work area.

Pick up the slices of bread and lay them on the chopping board side by side.

Open the tub of butter-like spread.

Pick up the knife and get some butter on the knife.

Spread the butter on the bread.

Put the knife down.

Pick up the pot of your favourite sandwich filling.

Open the pot.

Pick up the teaspoon and dip it into the pot then take out a spoonful of filling.

Put the spread on the bread.

Pick up the knife and use it to cover the bread with the filling.

Put down the knife and put the lid on the pot.

Pick up one slice of the bread and place it on top of the other slice of bread.

Pick up the knife and use the knife to cut the bread into four quarters.

Put the four small sandwiches onto the plate.

Take the plate to the table and put it on the table with the napkin.

Making a Popoid Figure

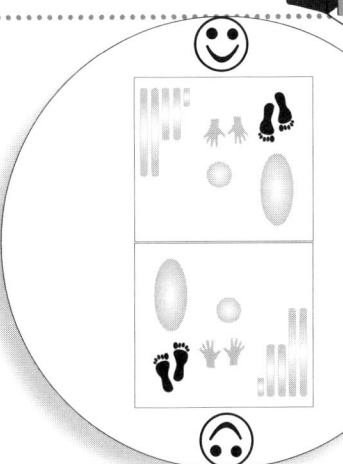

Equipment

- two heads
- two bodies
- two pairs of shoes or feet
- two hands
- ten connectors.

Script

Pick up the body and place one connector in the top hole to make a neck.

Pick up the head and put it on the connector used to make a neck.

Pick up one connector and extend it.

Place the extended connector into one side hole on the body.

Pick up a hand and place it on the end of the extended connector.

Pick up another connector, extend this connector and put it in the hole on the opposite side of the body then add the hand.

Pick up a connector and extend it.

Place the connector in one of the lower holes on the body.

Pick up a shoe or foot and place it on the end of the lower connector.

Pick up the last connector and extend it.

Place the extended connector in the remaining lower hole on the body.

Pick up a shoe or foot and place it on the end of the last connector.

Trying on a Hat

Equipment

- two large free standing mirrors

- two decorative hats.

Script

(Teacher and child sit side by side in front of the mirrors.)

Pick up the hat.

Place the hat on your head.

Look in the mirror and smile.

Re-arrange the hat on your head.

Look in the mirror and smile.

Making a Cup of Coffee

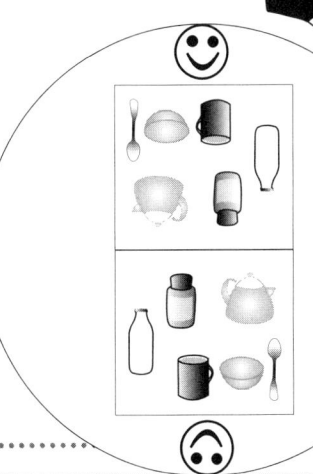

Equipment

- two electric kettles
- two mugs
- two jars of coffee
- two cartons of milk
- two teaspoons
- two bowls of sugar
- access to an electrical socket
- access to a cold water tap.

Script

Take the kettle to the cold water tap and fill it with water.

Take the kettle to the electrical socket and plug the kettle in to the socket then switch the power on. While the kettle is boiling return to work area.

Unscrew the jar of coffee.

Pick up the teaspoon and use it to take one spoonful of coffee from the jar.

Put the coffee into the mug.

Screw the top back onto the jar of coffee.

Use the teaspoon to get one spoon of sugar from the sugar bowl.

Put the sugar into the mug.

Go and collect the kettle of boiling water.

Switch off the power and unplug the kettle.

Lift the kettle up and carry it carefully back to the work area
(HEALTH WARNING: CHILDREN AND STUDENTS NEED TO BE TOLD THAT CARRYING BOILING WATER CAN BE DANGEROUS AND THEY NEED TO BE VERY CAREFUL.)

Carefully pour the water into the mug.

Take the kettle back to the work area and place it carefully on the work surface.

Return to the mug of coffee.

Open the carton of milk.

Pour the milk into the mug of coffee. Put the carton down away from the mug.

Pick up the teaspoon, place it in the mug of coffee and stir the coffee.

The coffee is now ready for you to drink – enjoy!

Exploring emotions with Teddy

Many young children and even some older children enjoy playing with soft toys. Soft toys can be used to increase the child's range of play experiences in a number of ways:

- exploring emotions

- practising verbs – make teddy jump, make teddy run, etc.

- re-enacting everyday experiences – feeding teddy, putting teddy to bed, taking teddy for a walk in a pushchair, etc.

- talking to teddy

- dressing teddy

- practising life skills, for example, doing up a variety of fastenings, zips, buttons, laces, etc.

Exploring Emotions with Teddy

Equipment

- two teddies.

Script

'Teddy is going for a walk.' (Walk the teddy along the carpet.)

'Teddy trips and falls.' (Drop the teddy to the carpet.)

'Teddy starts to cry.' (Make the sound of crying.)

'Pick teddy up and give it a cuddle.' (Hug the teddy.)

'Poor teddy, he is hurt.' (Rock the teddy in your arms.)

'Teddy is sad, he has hurt his leg.' (Continue to rock the tidy.)

'Teddy is feeling better, he has stopped crying and wants to play.'

(Walk the teddy and it along the carpet.)

Using Musical Instruments

Many children with ASDs may be fascinated by musical instruments. However, they may not use these in the usual way. For example, a child was observed playing with a rainmaker. He was very involved in the activity, holding the rainmaker close to his eyes and watching each of the beads dropping through the plastic platforms encased in the plastic shell of the rainmaker.

Equipment

• two tambours or tambourines
(any musical instruments can be used).

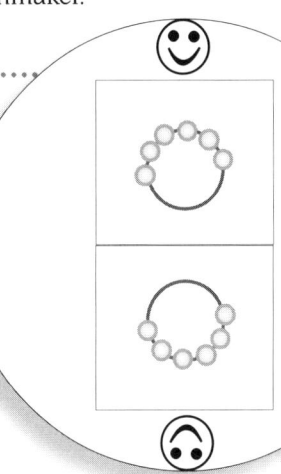

Script

Pick up the tambour and tap it; say, 'Tapping.'

(Repeat the action.)

Scratch your finger nails in a circular movement around the 'skin' of the tambour; say, 'Swirling.'

Beat out a simple rhythm and say, 'One, two, three, stop.'
Repeat several times, saying the words rhythmically.

Say, 'Tap, tap, tap, swirl, swirl, tap, tap, tap.' (Play your tambour as you give the instructions.)

Continue creating a variety of musical patterns.

Top Tips

Over time, it is possible to develop this idea into a musical conversation – the child or adult beating out a rhythm to which their partner responds by beating out a rhythm in reply.

Encouraging Conversation

Many children and young people experience great difficulty holding a conversation. It may be possible to begin to develop this skill through the use of telephones. In addition to this the child or young person can be taught the sequence used when making or receiving a telephone call.

Equipment

- two telephones
- two telephone directories
- two pencils
- two notebooks.

Please Note:

It is important to note the context in which such a telephone conversation is likely to take place. The situation presented below has been used to teach a young student to answer the telephone during a school lunch break.

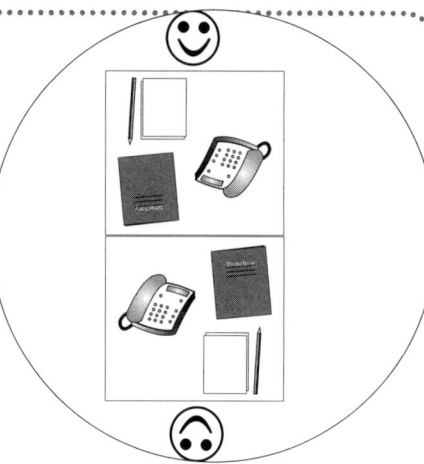

Script

(If it is possible set the telephones to ring, if this is not possible make a tape of the sound of a ringing telephone or use your voice to emulate the sound.)

Pick up the receiver of the telephone and say, 'Hello, who would you like to speak to?'

Say, 'I'm sorry, ..., is not available at the moment, can I take a message?'

Use the notebook to write down the message – as you write, say what you are writing. 'Please ask .... to call ....'

'Thank you for calling. I will give the message to .... when they return to their class.'

(Replace the telephone receiver, remove the page from the notebook which contains the message and place it to one side.)

Top Tips

Telephones and telephone directories can be used to put the following skills into meaningful contexts:

- the teaching of alphabetical order
- number recognition and recall
- making a call to the emergency service.

Section 6

Powerpoint Slides

Teaching Play to Children with Autistic Spectrum Disorders

Using Indentiplay

A Lucky Duck Publication
Paul Chapman Publishing

Nicky Phillips and Liz Beavan

Play in children with ASD is often described as:

- repetitive
- motoric
- sensory
- isolated
- purposeless
- lacking in imagination.

Nicky Phillips and Liz Beavan

Play relies on:

- language
- social interaction and social understanding
- flexibility and imagination
- social experience and interest in social behaviour.

Nicky Phillips and Liz Beavan

Why Play?

- All children need play skills if they are to be included – children need to experience peer interactions.
- Play is a tool for learning; all children need this opportunity.
- All children need to practise social routines in safe surroundings.
- It's fun!

Nicky Phillips and Liz Beavan

Why Play?

- cognition
- social skills
- language
- problem-solving
- emotional development.

Nicky Phillips and Liz Beavan

What is Identiplay?

A structured play intervention that includes:

- a shared focus
- imitation
- parallel play
- play dialogue
- narrative structure in the form of play scripts
- flexibility.

Nicky Phillips and Liz Beavan

You will need:

- A table divided in two (with a clear area for the child's toys and a clear area for the adult's toys).
- Two chairs, usually facing one another, on either side of the table.
- A pack containing two identical sets of toys.
- A typed script detailing the layout of the toys and what the adult will say and do with the toys.

Nicky Phillips and Liz Beavan

Before starting Identiplay:

- Assess the child's play skills and find the right level.
- Choose toys appropriate to the skills level of the child.
- Set up the table, chairs and toys.
- Let the child explore the toys.

Nicky Phillips and Liz Beavan

References

Beyer, J. and Gammeltoft, L. (2000) *Autism and Play*. London: Jessica Kingsley.

Cumine, J., Leach, J. and Stevenson, G. (2001) *Autism in the Early Years, A practical guide*. London: Fulton.

Jordan, R. and Jones, G. (2001) *Meeting the Needs of Children with Autistic Spectrum Disorders*. London: Fulton.

Libby, S., Powell, S., Messer, D. and Jordan, R. (1997) *Imitation of Pretend Play Acts by Children with Autistic Spectrum Disorders and Downs Syndrome*. Journal of Autsim and Developmental Disorders. 27, 365-383.

Neaum, S. and Tallack, J. (1997) *Good Practice in Implementing the Pre-school Curriculum*. London: Nelson Thornes.

Rubin, K., Fein, G. and Vandenberg, B. (1983) *Play*. in Mussen, P.H. & Hetherington, E.M. (eds) Carmichael's Manual of Child Psychology. Vol 3, 4th ed. New York: Wiley.

Sheratt, D. (1999) *The Importance of Play*. Good Autism Practice. September, 23-41.

Sherratt, D. and Peter, M. (2002) *Developing Play and Drama in Children with Autistic Spectrum Disorders*. London: Fulton.

Schopler, E., Mesibov, G.B. and Hearsey, K.A. (1995) *Structured Teaching in the TEACCH System* in Schopler, E. & Mesibov, G.B. (eds) Learning and Cognition in Autism. New York: Plenum Press.

Thomas, N. and Smith, C. (2004) *Developing Play in Children with Autistic Spectrum Disorders*. Educational Psychology in Practice. Vol 20, 3, 195-206.

Thornton, K. and Cox, E. (2005) *Play and the reduction of challenging behaviour in children with ASD and learning disabilities*. Good Autism Practice. 6,2, 75-80.

Ungerer, J. and Sigman, M. (1981) *Symbolic Play and Language Comprehension in autistic children*. Journal of the American Academy of Child Psychiatry, 20, 318-337.

Williams, D. (1998) *Like Colour to the Blind*. London: Jessica Kingsley.

Wing, L. and Attwood, A. (1987) *Syndromes of Autism and Atypical Development* in Cohen, C. & Donnellan, A. (eds), Handbook of Autism and Pervasive Developmental Disorders. New York: Wiley.

Wolfberg, P. J. (1999) *Play and Imagination in Children with Autism*. New York: Teachers College Press.